PEGASUS ENCYCLOPEDIA LIBRARY

Natural Disaster
HURRICANE

Edited by: Pallabi B. Tomar, Hitesh Iplani
Managing editor: Tapasi De
Designed by: Vijesh Chahal, Anil Kumar, Rohit Kumar
Illustrated by: Suman S. Roy, Tanoy Choudhury
Colouring done by: Vinay Kumar, Kiran Kumari & Pradeep Kumar

CONTENTS

What is a hurricane? 3

History of hurricanes 5

How hurricanes form 6

Hurricane structure 8

Causes of hurricanes 9

Stages of development 11

Hurricane categories: The Saffir-Simpson Scale...... 14

When and where do hurricanes occur? 16

Damages 17

Tracking of hurricanes.. 19

Naming hurricanes 21

Some hurricane terms 22

Better safe than sorry 23

Deadliest hurricanes in history 24

Test Your Memory..31

Index 32

What is a hurricane?

Hurricanes are violent, powerful storms which mainly carry strong winds and heavy rains and can destroy anything that comes its way. Hurricanes occur in particular seasons.

A hurricane can be defined as a **spiral storm**, which initiates in a sea near the equator and travels to the shore in a powerful pace. Hurricanes bring along strong stormy winds (which are more than 119 km/h), heavy rains and huge waves with them, that crash fiercely on the land they hit. They can destroy vast amount of property and life when they hit land.

All hurricanes begin in a warm moist atmosphere over tropical ocean waters.

HURRICANE

There have been hurricanes in every year in the last five centuries. And each year has witnessed at least one great hurricane. These huge storms begin in the tropics over the oceans. Hurricanes are referred to by different labels depending on where they occur. They are called **hurricanes** when they happen over the North Atlantic Ocean, the Caribbean Sea, the Gulf of Mexico, or the north-east Pacific Ocean. Such storms are known as **typhoons** if they occur in the north-west Pacific Ocean, west of an imaginary line called the International Date Line. Near Australia and in the Indian Ocean, they are referred to as **tropical cyclones**. Locals also give these storms different names. In Australia, for example, residents call them willy-willies.

> Hurricanes can also produce tornadoes. They are not as strong as regular tornadoes and last only a few minutes.

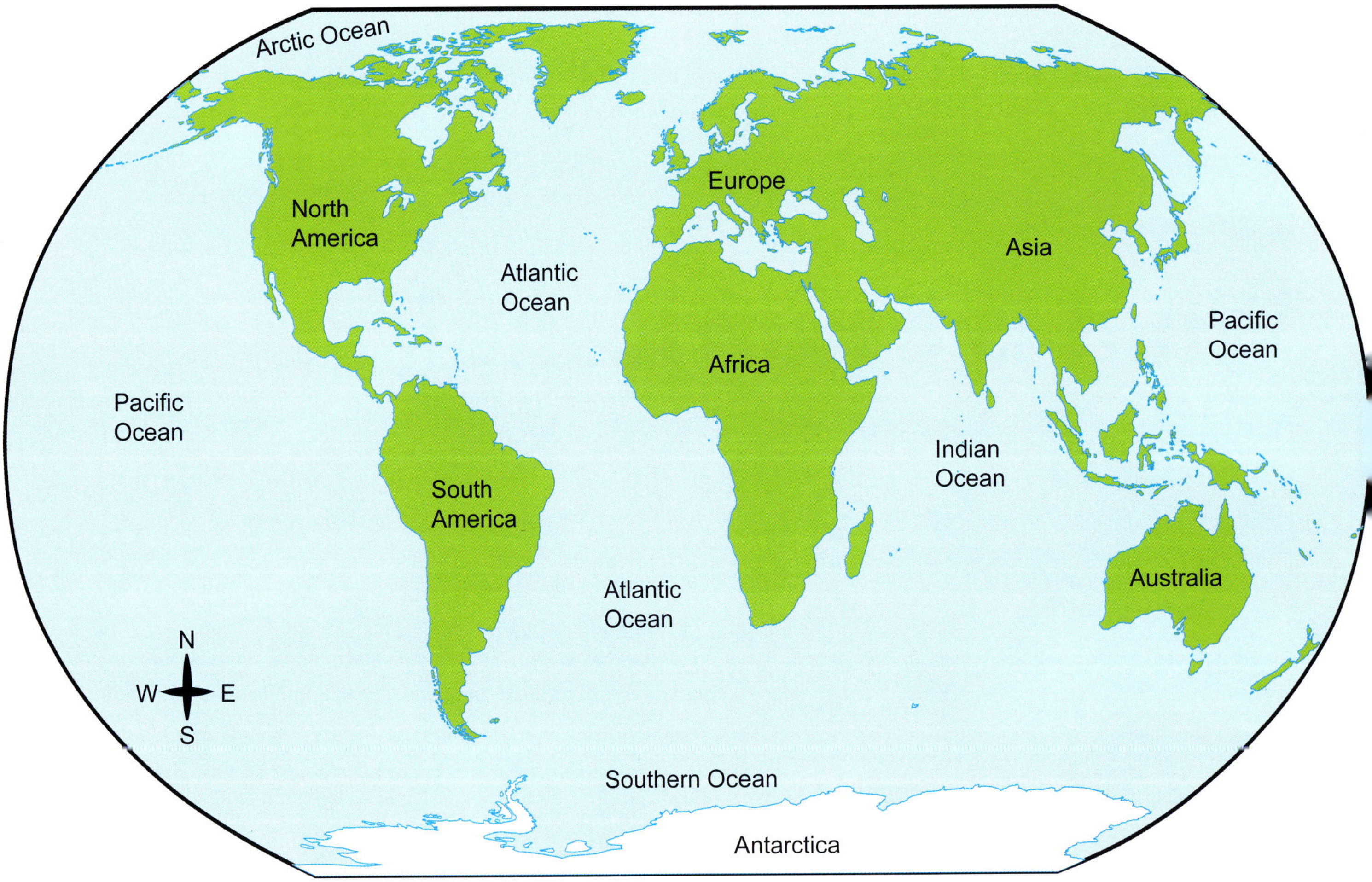

The Oceans World Map

History of hurricanes

Scientists have only been studying hurricanes only for about 100 years. But there is evidence of hurricanes occurring long in the past. For example, geologists believe that layers of sediment in a lake in Alabama were brought there by a hurricane in the Gulf of Mexico as long as 3,000 years ago! There is also evidence in Florida of hurricanes occurring more than 1,000 years ago.

The Central American Mayas believed the storm to be Huracan, a god of large winds and evil spirits. Spanish explorers roaming the region learned his name from the natives and the word later became today's 'hurricane'.

Many storms left important marks in history. In 1565, a hurricane scattered a French fleet of war ships and allowed the Spanish to capture a French fort in what is now Florida. In 1609, a fleet of ships carrying settlers from England to Virginia was struck by a hurricane. Some of the ships were damaged and part of the fleet grounded on Bermuda, an island nation in the Atlantic. These passengers became the first people to live on Bermuda. In 1640, a hurricane partially destroyed a large Dutch fleet that was waiting to attack Cuba.

Astonishing fact

Every second, a large hurricane releases the energy of 10 atomic bombs.

How hurricanes form

During the summer months, the sun's radiation beats down continuously on the ocean waters in the tropics. As a result, warm air rises and drifts skyward. Cooler air from above takes the place of rising, warm air. This is known as a convection cycle. Storms that form north of the equator spin counterclockwise. Storms south of the equator spin clockwise. This difference is because of Earth's rotation on its axis.

As the warm air continues to rise in the convection cycle, the atmospheric pressure falls making the winds blow stronger.

Before a hurricane is able to develop, the ocean waters must have a surface temperature of at least 80°F. Air near the oceans surface must contain a lot of moisture. Finally, winds must be converging which means coming together from different directions.

Astonishing fact

Slow moving hurricanes produce more rainfall and can cause more damage from flooding than faster-moving, more powerful hurricanes.

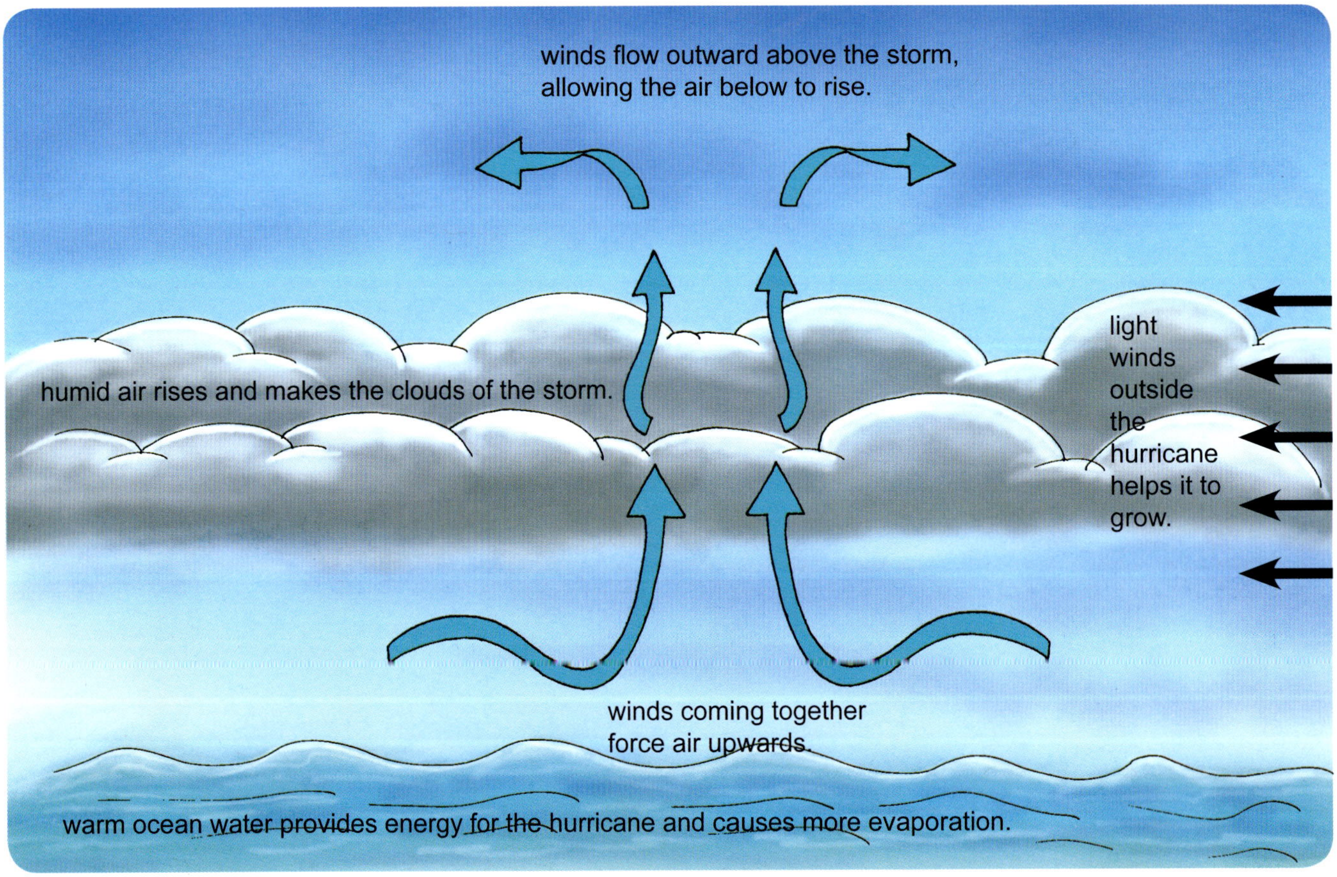

Formation of a hurricane

How hurricanes form

Once formed, hurricanes take energy from the warm ocean water to become stronger. A storm will strengthen if there is a supply of warm, moist air to feed it. Warm, moist air is found above warm, tropical ocean waters. While a hurricane is over warm water it will continue to grow. A hurricane dies when it moves away from the tropics. When a hurricane moves into areas with cooler ocean water, it weakens. It will also weaken if it travels over land.

The rotation of the storm is due to the **Coriolis Effect**, a natural phenomenon that causes fluids and free-moving objects to turn to the right of their destination in the Northern Hemisphere and to the left in the Southern Hemisphere. This causes the air being drawn into the central low pressure to curve. The air rises as it rotates. This rising air, which is saturated with water, cools and condenses, forming clouds. Hurricanes do not occur within 500 kilometres of the equator because there is no Coriolis Effect at the equator.

Astonishing fact

The planet Jupiter has a hurricane which has been going on for over 300 years! It can be seen as a red spot on the planet. This hurricane on Jupiter is bigger than the Earth itself.

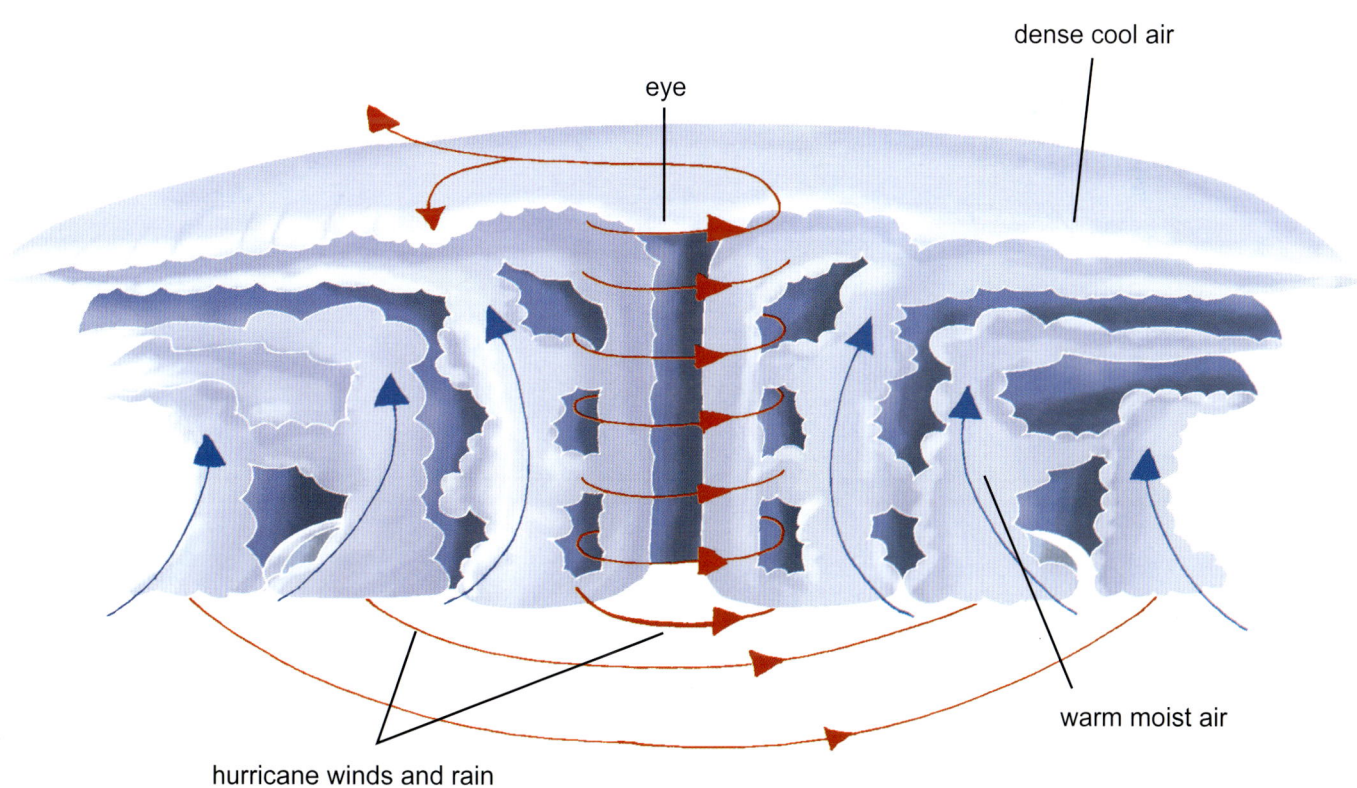

dense cool air

eye

warm moist air

hurricane winds and rain

Hurricane structure

Hurricane winds blow in a counterclockwise spiral around the calm, roughly circular centre called the **eye**. In the eye, which is roughly 32-48km wide, it is relatively calm and there is little or no rain. The eye is the warmest part of the storm.

Surrounding the eye is the eyewall, a wall of thunderclouds. The eyewall has the most rain and the strongest winds of the storm, gusting up to 360 km/h in severe storms. The smaller the eye, the stronger are the winds. The winds spiral in a counterclockwise direction into the storm's low-pressure centre.

Long bands of rain clouds appear to spiral inward to the eyewall These are called **spiral rainbands**. Hurricanes can stretch for hundreds of miles.

In addition to rotating with wind speeds of at least 119 km/h, a hurricane travels relatively slowly across the ocean or land, usually at about 32-40km/h.

If you are facing in the direction that the hurricane is travelling, the right side generally has the fastest winds and the left side usually has the most rain.

> The Great Colonial Hurricane of 1635 was the first recorded to hit New England.

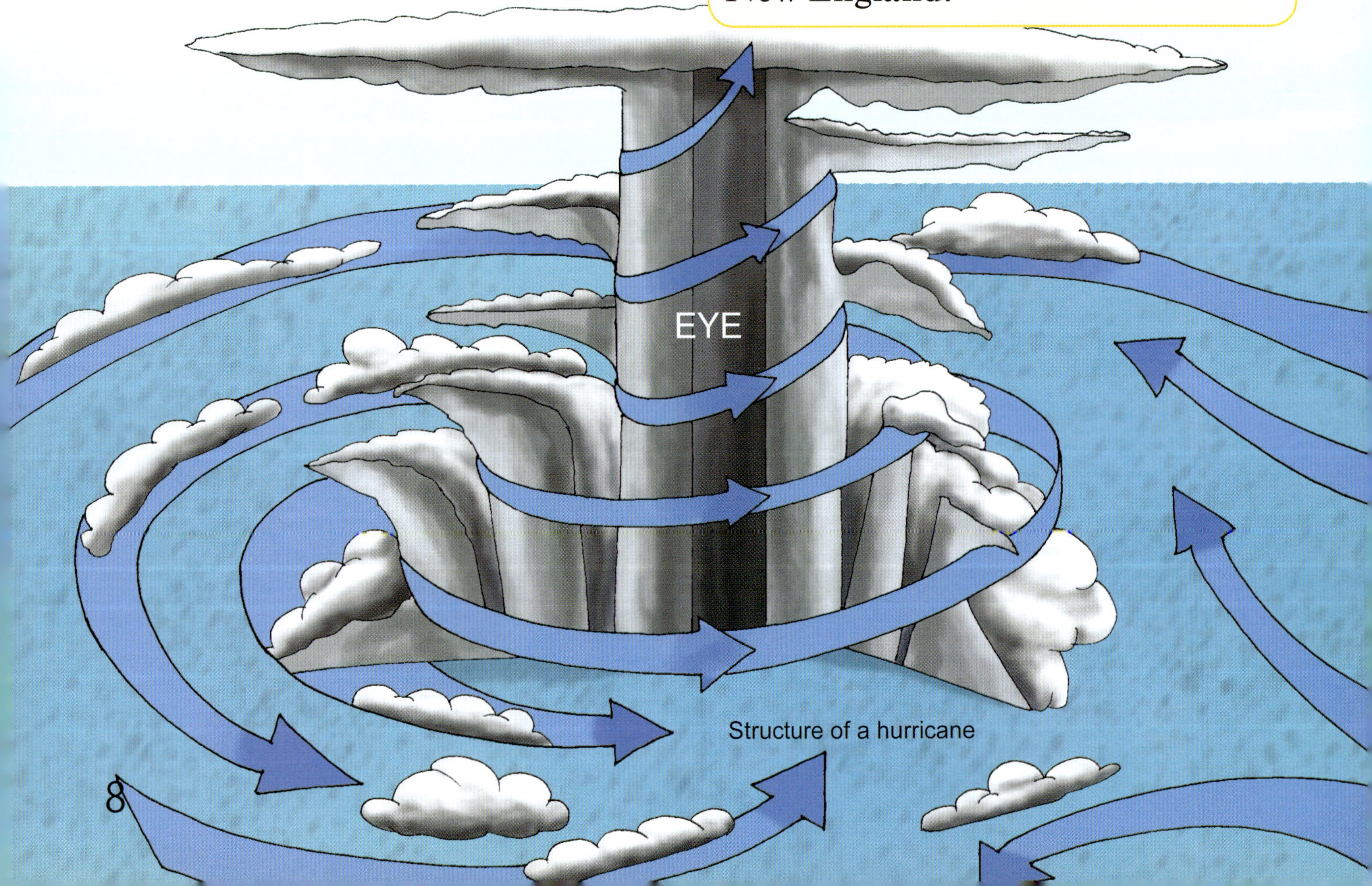

Structure of a hurricane

Causes of hurricanes

Hurricanes are also known as tropical cyclones or typhoons depending on the location. They are some of the most powerful storms in nature. They can have winds that exceed 100 km/h and cause massive flooding. When a hurricane passes over populated areas it can cause billions in damage. In the case of Hurricane Katrina an entire major American city was flooded.

> **Most people who die in hurricanes are killed by the towering walls of sea water that comes inland.**

The cause of a hurricane is low pressure and warm water. In the Atlantic Ocean most hurricanes are born from tropical storms generated by the warm waters off the African coast. This warm water evaporates and becomes water vapour. This evaporation causes a difference in air pressure between the different regions of the atmosphere designated as low pressure and high pressure. Changes in air pressure help direct weather worldwide. An area of low pressure can push a storm towards one region instead of another.

HURRICANE

When the tropical storm is first created it is still just a normal storm over the sea. However, if the water remains warm it becomes fuel making the storm to gradually grow stronger. As more water is evaporated and added to the storm the difference in pressure becomes more pronounced creating an area of low pressure. This low pressure area draws the storm system into a spiral around itself creating a hurricane. The low pressure area becomes the eye of the hurricane and the band of clouds immediately around it becomes the eye wall.

The truly destructive part of the hurricane is the eye wall. This is because this is where the most powerful winds are located. The greater the difference in pressure the more powerful and destructive the eye wall becomes. This is why meteorologists pay attention to the barometer readings on tropical storms. If the air pressure drops drastically it normally foretells a particularly strong hurricane. Another factor that can affect the strength of forming hurricanes is **El Nino**. This is a weather phenomenon in which the waters off the western coast of South America become unusually warm. The occurrence of this event helps to determine particularly for North America if there will be a lot of strong hurricanes.

Stages of development

Hurricanes go through a process of development that involves several different stages. These stages can have different lengths depending on certain environmental conditions where it is located at a particular time. If these conditions are right, a hurricane can develop rapidly, and go through these early stages very quickly. If these conditions aren't right, then development can be slow or not at all. Here are the various stages of development a hurricane goes through.

Tropical disturbance

Tropical disturbance is an area where rain clouds are building. The clouds form when moist air rises and becomes cooler. Cool air cannot hold as much water vapour as warm air can, and the excess water changes into tiny droplets of water that form clouds. The clouds in a tropical disturbance may rise to great heights, forming the towering thunderclouds that meteorologists call **cumulonimbus clouds**.

Cumulonimbus clouds usually produce heavy rains that end after an hour or two, and the weather clears rapidly. If conditions are right for a hurricane, however, there is so much heat energy and moisture in the atmosphere that new cumulonimbus clouds continually form from rising moist air.

Developement of a hurricane

A typical hurricane can give 6 inches to a foot of rain across a region.

HURRICANE

Tropical depression

Tropical depression is a low-pressure area surrounded by winds that have begun to blow in a circular pattern. A meteorologist considers a depression to exist when there is low pressure over a large enough area to be plotted on a weather map. The low pressure near the ocean surface draws in warm, moist air, which feeds more thunderstorms.

The winds swirl slowly around the low-pressure area at first. As the pressure becomes even lower, warmer, moist air is drawn in, and the winds blow faster.

Tropical storm

When the winds exceed 61 km per hour, a tropical storm develops. Viewed from above, the storm clouds now have a well-defined circular shape. The seas become so rough that ships must steer clear of that area. The strong winds near the surface of the ocean draw more and more heat and water vapour from the sea. The increased warmth and moisture in the air feed the storm.

A tropical storm has a column of warm air near its centre. The warmer this column becomes, the more the pressure at the surface falls. The falling pressure, in turn, draws more air into the storm. As more air is pulled into the storm, the winds blow harder.

Astonishing fact

The 1899 Bathhurst Bay Hurricane in the South Pacific caused a storm surge of 12 m, the highest ever recorded!

Stages of development

Hurricane

A storm achieves hurricane status when its winds exceed 119 km per hour. By the time a storm reaches hurricane intensity, it usually has a well-developed eye at its centre. Surface pressure drops to its lowest in the eye.

In the eyewall, warm air spirals upward creating the hurricane's strongest winds. The speed of the winds in the eyewall is related to the diametre of the eye. Just as ice skaters spin faster when they pull their arms in, a hurricane's winds blow faster if its eye is small. If the eye widens, the winds decrease.

Heavy rains fall come from the eyewall and bands of dense clouds swirl around the eyewall. These bands, called rainbands, can produce more than 2 inches of rain per hour. The hurricane draws large amounts of heat and moisture from the sea.

Astonishing fact

Florida has had more hurricanes than any other state. Over 60 have touched down there since 1900.

Hurricane categories: The Saffir-Simpson Scale

There are various scales put forth by experts to measure the intensity of the hurricane. The Saffir-Simpson Hurricane Scale was developed by a meteorologist Bob Simpson and civil engineer Herbert Saffir in 1971. The Saffir-Simpson Hurricane Scale categorizes hurricanes on a scale of 1 to 5. It's based on the storm's intensity. The scale is used to give an estimate of the potential damage a hurricane can do to property and the flooding it may bring in coastal areas.

Category 1

In this category, storms sustain winds of 119-153 km/h, while the storm surge is around 1 m. These hurricanes usually don't cause any major damage to buildings. But they are powerful enough to uproot or snap trees. They can also topple unanchored mobile homes. In 2008, Hurricane Hanna was a category 1 hurricane.

Category 2

Category 2 hurricanes produce wind with speeds of 154-177 km/h and storm surges of generally 1-2 m above normal. Damage to permanent structures includes wind damage to roofing and some window damage. Some trees can be blown down and coastal escape routes should be avoided as they may be dangerously flooded. Small crafts left in the water may break away from their moorings.

Herbert Saffir

Bob simpson on left

> The Saffir-Simpson Hurricane Scale was developed by meteorologist Bob Simpson and a civil engineer named Herbert Saffir, in 1971.

Hurricane Categories: The Saffir-Simpson Scale

Category 3

Category 3 hurricanes produce wind speeds of 178-209 km/h and storm surges that are 2-3 m above normal. Damage to small buildings beyond broken windows and roofs is possible and temporary structures are totally destroyed. Large trees maybe blown down and foliage that has been blown off trees can become hazardous debris.

Category 4

With continuous winds around 210-249 km/h, these hurricanes create havoc in fairly populated areas. Mobile homes and normal homes are levelled in such a situation. The huge storm surge, in case of category 4 hurricanes, is 3-5 m. Roofs of buildings may also undergo major damage.

Category 5

According to the Saffir-Simpson Scale, this is the peak a tropical cyclone can reach. Category 5 hurricanes produce wind speeds greater than 249 km/h and storm surges generally greater than 5 m above normal. With these high speed winds, most modern residential structures can be severely damaged. All trees and street signs will be completely blown away and windows and doors will be completely destroyed. Storm surges will cause extensive damage to the lower floors of buildings located less then 4 m above sea-level and within 500 yards of shoreline.

> Two hurricanes were named Alice in 1954 which occured one in June and one in December.

Saffir–Simpson Hurricane Scale

Category	Wind speed (km/h)	Storm surge (m)
Five	249 km/h	greater than 5 m above normal
Four	210-249 km/h	3-5 m
Three	178-209 km/h	storm surges that are 2-3 m
Two	154-177 km/h	1-2 m
One	119-153 km/h	storm surge is around 1 m

When and where do hurricanes occur?

Hurricanes are by far the most common in the Pacific Ocean, with the western Pacific being most active. Below is a brief description of each basin's hurricane season.

ATLANTIC: Hurricane season in the Atlantic runs from June 1 to November 30. Storms outside these dates are not unheard of.

Astonishing fact

Hurricane Floyd was barely a category I hurricane, but it still managed to mow down 19 million trees and caused over a billion dollars in damage!

EASTERN PACIFIC: The Eastern Pacific basin's hurricane season is from May 15th to November 30th, peaking in late August to early September.

WESTERN PACIFIC: The Western Pacific basin's hurricane season is mostly from July 1 to November 30, peaking in late August or early September though storms can occur year-round.

SOUTH PACIFIC: The South Pacific basin's hurricane season is from October 15 to May 15, reaching a peak in late February or early March.

INDIAN OCEAN: The Indian basin's hurricane season is from April 1 to December 31 for the northern Indian Ocean and from October 15 to May 31 in the southern region.

Damages

Hurricanes are the most devastating natural disaster, effecting thousands of people each year. During each hurricane season, innocent people are injured, property is demolished, and money is forever lost. Hurricanes cause damage in a variety of ways, including strong winds, storm surges, flooding, tornadoes, and rip tides.

Strong winds

The strong winds of a hurricane are most often associated with the widespread damage from a hurricane. The rapidly moving winds can uproot trees; throw cars, and level buildings. A storm is first classified as a hurricane when its winds exceed 119 km/h, though many reach as dangerously high as 321 km/h.

Storm surges

The most dangerous effect of a hurricane is a rapid rise in sea level called a storm surge. A storm surge is produced when winds drive ocean waters ashore. Storm surges are dangerous because many coastal areas are densely populated and lie only a few feet or metres above sea level. A 1970 a cyclone in East Pakistan (now Bangladesh) produced a surge that killed about 266,000 people. A hurricane in Galveston, Texas, in 1900 produced a surge that killed about 6,000 people, the worst natural disaster in United States' history.

Astonishing fact

In 1967, a hurricane in Texas caused more than 140 twisters!

Flooding

Flooding is caused by the storm surges and the heavy rainfall associated with the storm. Even when the hurricane moves inland and begins to deteriorate, there still may be a tremendous amount of rainfall.

Tornadoes

Many people are unaware of tornadoes that form during hurricanes. These tornadoes are found relatively close to the eye wall of a hurricane where the conditions are ideal for their formation. The tornadoes occur in heavy areas of rain, making them extremely difficult to track.

Riptides

Riptides are the final source of damage from hurricanes. Rip tides are very powerful sea currents moving outward from the shore when a strong storm is nearby. They are formed by the strong winds pushing water toward the shore, similar to storm surges. Winds from tropical cyclones push waves up against the shoreline even if the storm is hundreds of miles away, making rip tides the first indications of an approaching hurricane.

Astonishing fact

In 1989, Hurricane Hugo completely destroyed several forests in South Carolina.

Tracking of hurricanes

Hurricane tracking is an evolving science that uses various methods and devices to gather information about a hurricane. Information gathered from the devices is used by the National Hurricane Centre to forecast the track and intensity of a storm.

Four major methods currently being used to track hurricanes are **satellite imagery, Doppler radar, reconnaissance aircraft** and **observational equipment**.

Satellite images give information about the track and development of a hurricane, while Doppler radar provides rainfall estimates and portrays the rain bands, eye wall and eye of the hurricane. Reconnaissance aircraft are flown into the eye of the hurricane by both the National Oceanic and Atmospheric Administration (NOAA) and the Air Force Reserve to gather data, including pressure, eye location and storm size. Observational equipment such as data buoys relay pertinent information as well.

The first U.S. satellite to monitor weather conditions was TIROS, launched in 1960. The US Weather Service initiated a national hurricane warning system toward the end of the 20th century.

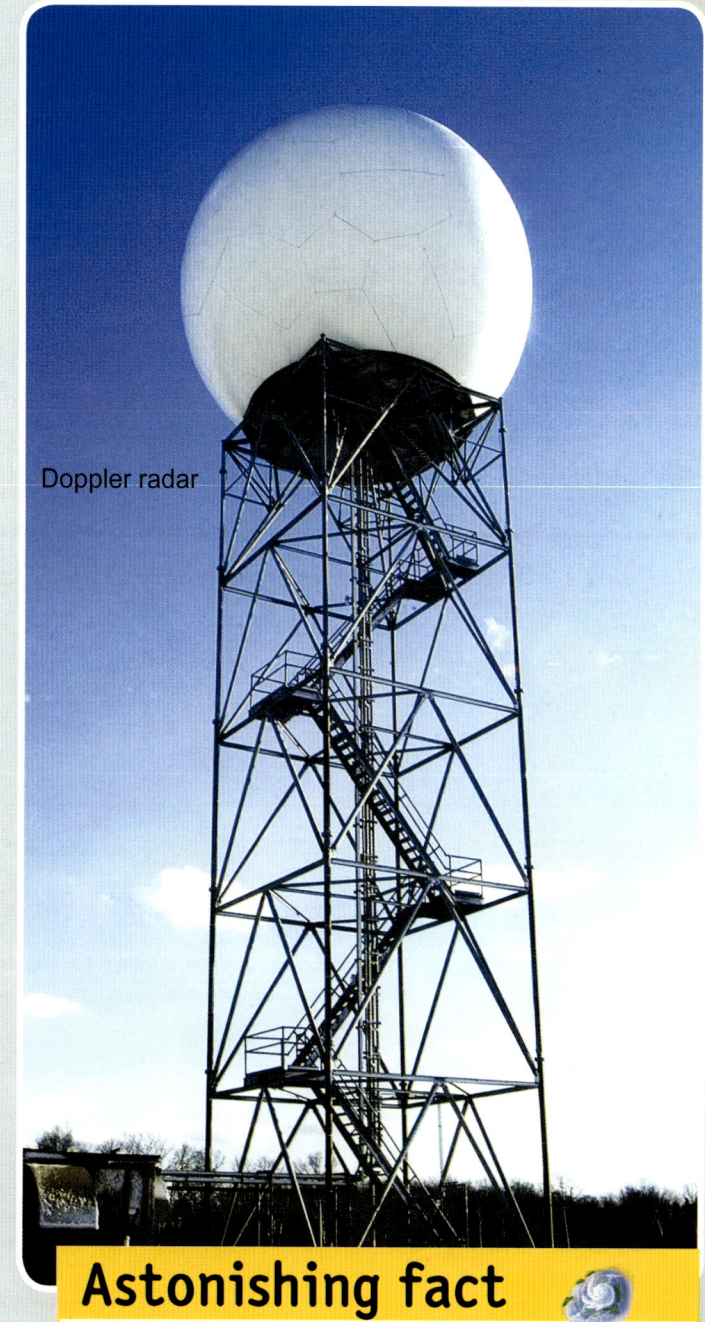

Doppler radar

Astonishing fact

In 1944, the US Navy's Pacific fleet was crushed by Typhoon Cobra, which sank three destroyers and damaged many ships.

HURRICANE

Modern technology provides forecasters with the ability to accurately determine the position and intensity of hurricanes. This information is used to provide advanced warnings to those populations at risk. If it appears that a particular area is in potential danger of being struck by a hurricane, a 'hurricane watch' is issued, sometimes up to several days in advance of the storm's predicted arrival. When there is a high probability that a hurricane will strike an area within 24 hours, a 'hurricane warning' is issued. Unfortunately, despite the advanced warning systems, hurricanes still claim the lives of hundreds, even thousands of people each year.

Hurricane hunters

The brave 'hurricane hunters' work for the National Oceanic and Atmospheric Administration (NOAA). Each mission lasts about ten hours, with the crews passing four to six times through the storm. The planes carry radar, sophisticated computers, and weather instruments that determine characteristics such as temperature, air pressure, wind speed, and wind direction inside the hurricane. The crews also release instruments that measure temperature, air pressure, and wind at different levels as the devices drop through the hurricane toward the ocean. By mission's end, NOAA can warn everyone in the hurricane's path.

Astonishing fact

In 1970, a hurricane in Pakistan killed more than 300,000 people.

Astonishing fact

In 1971, Hurricane Ginger lasted for over three weeks.

Hurricane Hunters

Naming hurricanes

Once modern hurricane tracking systems began, scientists found it necessary to identify each storm. Beginning in 1953, the first storm of the season was given a woman's name starting with the letter A. The second storm was a woman's name beginning with the letter B, and so on. It wasn't until 1979 that men's names began to be used.

Every six years, the names repeat. However, if the storm was particularly violent or destructive, the name is taken off the list. That way, when someone mentions Hurricane Camille, most people know they mean the storm that hit the Mississippi Delta in 1969.

Sometimes, names are specially changed to suit the area of the world that is hit. When hurricanes approach within 1,000 miles of Hawaii, for example, they are given Hawaiian names.

Hurricanes are assigned with different names, depending upon the area where they have occurred. Hurricane storms are called hurricanes, if they start over the Caribbean Sea, the north-east Pacific Ocean and the North Atlantic Ocean; whereas storms are called tropical cyclones if they occur in the Indian Ocean or near Australia.

Some hurricane terms

Tropical storm watch - Tropical storm conditions with sustained winds from 62 -119 km/h is possible in your area within the next 36 hours.

Tropical storm warning - Tropical storm conditions are expected in your area within the next 24 hours.

Hurricane watch - Hurricane conditions with sustained winds of 119 km/h or greater are possible in your area within the next 36 hours. This watch should trigger your family's disaster plan, and protective measures should be initiated.

Hurricane warning - Hurricane conditions are expected in your area within 24 hours. Once this warning has been issued, your family should be in the process of completing protective actions and deciding the safest location to be during the storm.

Coastal flood watch - The possibility exists for the inundation of land areas along the coast within the next 12 to 36 hours.

Coastal flood warning - Land areas along the coast are expected to become inundated by sea water above the typical tide action.

Better safe than sorry

Hurricane safety tips

Hurricane is a tropical cyclone that moves with heavy rains and high winds. These natural disasters can be very devastating. If you are prepared before hand, loss can actually be avoided or at least minimized.

Before a hurricane: Have a disaster plan ready. Board up windows and bring in outdoor objects that could blow away. Make sure you know which county or parish you live in and know where all the evacuation routes are.

Prepare a disaster supplies kit for your home and car. Include a first aid kit, canned food and a can opener, bottled water, battery-operated radio, flashlight, protective clothing and written instructions on how to turn off electricity, gas, and water. Have a radio handy with plenty of batteries, so you can listen to storm advisories. Have some cash handy as well, because following a hurricane, banks and ATMs maybe closed. Make sure your car is filled with fuel.

During a hurricane: Stay away from low-lying and flood prone areas. Always stay indoors during a hurricane, because strong winds will blow things around. If your home isn't on higher ground, go to a shelter. If emergency managers say to evacuate, then do so immediately.

After a hurricane: Stay indoors until it is safe to come out. Check for injured or trapped people, without putting yourself in danger. Watch out for flooding which can happen after a hurricane. Do not attempt to drive in flooding water. Stay away from standing water. It maybe electrically charged from underground or downed power lines. Don't drink tap water until officials say it's safe to do so.

> Hurricanes do not occur in the South Atlantic Ocean, where the waters are too cold for them to form.

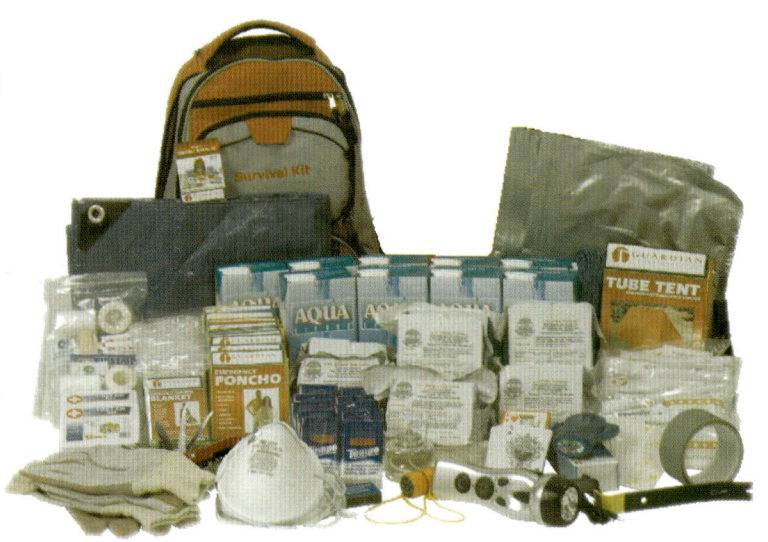

Hurricane safety kit

Deadliest hurricanes in history

Hurricane Katrina

Hurricane Katrina was the eleventh named tropical storm, third major hurricane, and first Category 5 hurricane of the 2005 Atlantic hurricane season. It first made landfall as a Category 1 hurricane just north of Miami, Florida on August 25, 2005, then again on August 29 along the Central Gulf Coast near New Orleans, Louisiana, as a Category 4 storm. Katrina resulted in breaches of the levee system that protected New Orleans from Lake Pontchartrain, and most of the city was subsequently flooded by the lake's waters. This and other major damage to the coastal regions of Louisiana, Mississippi, and Alabama made Katrina the most destructive and costliest natural disaster in the history of the United States.

By the time the hurricane subsided, Katrina had claimed more than 1,800 human lives and caused roughly $125 billion in damages.

Katrina was just one of 28 named tropical cyclones during the 2005 hurricane season, but due to the tragedy it caused, it remains the one most remembered. The World Meteorological Organization has since retired the name 'Katrina' from its list of hurricane names. As such, there will never be another Hurricane Katrina.

Deadliest hurricanes in history

Bhola cyclone

The Bhola cyclone and tidal surge occurred in East Pakistan (now Bangladesh) on November 13, 1970. It was one of the greatest tropical cyclones of the 20th century.

On the night of November 12, a tropical cyclone in the Bay of Bengal was approaching the coast of East Pakistan. Winds in excess of 190 km/h, combined with an exceptionally high tide of 5 to 6 m, drove a tidal surge into the low lying, densely populated region in the early hours of the morning. The result was widespread flooding, with many people being drowned in their sleep.

The official death toll was put at 500,000 with 100,000 people missing, making it the deadliest tropical cyclone on record. Many estimates put the figure higher. It is also one of the deadliest natural disasters in modern times, being comparable to the 1976 Tangshan earthquake and the 2004 Indian Ocean earthquake.

The highest loss of life and destruction occurred on the low lying islands of the Ganges Delta south of Dhaka. The island and district of Bhola (where casualties may have exceeded 100,000) was particularly impacted, with the towns of Charfasson and Tazumuddin being devastated. The city of Chittagong was also badly affected.

HURRICANE

Galveston Hurricane (1900)

On September 8, 1900, the greatest natural disaster to ever strike the United States occurred at Galveston, Texas. In the early evening hours of September 8, a hurricane came ashore at Galveston bringing with it a great storm surge that inundated most of Galveston Island and the city of Galveston. As a result, much of the city was destroyed and at least 6,000 people were killed in a few hours time.

The Galveston Hurricane of 1900, is the deadliest natural disaster ever to strike the United States, taking the lives of an estimated 8,000 - 12,000 people in and around the area of Galveston, Texas. The estimated sustained winds were 217km/h, making it a Category 4 storm on the Saffir-Simpson Scale. The city of Galveston was hit hard by high winds and up to 4 m storm surges. Much of the city was covered in water as the highest point in Galveston is not even 2 m above sea level. The surge knocked buildings off their foundations, and the surf pounded them to pieces. Over 3,600 homes were destroyed, and a wall of debris faced the ocean. The few buildings which survived are today maintained as tourist attractions. All said and done, Galveston lost approximately a fifth of its population!

Haiphong typhoon, Vietnam, 1881

Haiphong typhoon was one of most catastrophic natural disasters in history and the third deadliest tropical cyclone ever recorded. The cyclone smashed into the Gulf of Tonkin, setting off tidal waves that flooded the city of Haiphong in northeastern Vietnam, caused widespread destruction, and killed an estimated 300,000 inhabitants.

Haiphong, Vietnam, in the Gulf of Tonkin, lies directly in one of the most frequently used paths for those Pacific typhoons that originate in and around the Philippines and reach the Asian mainland through the Gulf of Tonkin. The typhoon that arrived on September 15, 1881, was very powerful and it devastated Haiphong and the surrounding coastal area. Three hundred thousand died. Little is known of the social and environmental conditions there at that time. It seems that no protective barriers were in place to protect people against a typhoon.

Bangladesh Cyclone (1991)

On the list of the world's deadliest tropical storms, the 1991 cyclone ranks ninth, taking nearly 140,000 lives. The storm struck on the night of April 29, 1991 in the Chittagong district of south-eastern Bangladesh.

The fiercest cyclone ever known around the Bay of Bengal struck Bangladesh on the night of 29 April 1991. It ripped across southern Chittagong with torrential rains, winds of around 250 km/h and a storm surge 6 m high, a combination that killed at least 138,000 people and left up to 10 million homeless. The cyclone unofficially named 'Gorky', made landfall as a Category 4 storm, bordering on Category 5. As a comparison, Hurricane Katrina was Category 3 when it hit similarly low-lying New Orleans in 2005.

The deadly combination of high storm winds and high storm surge hammered the coastline. A concrete levee (an embankment alongside a river to prevent high water from flooding bordering areas) erected near the mouth of the Karnaphuli River in Patenga to protect against storm surge washed away under the storm's onslaught. The winds lifted a 100-ton crane located in the Port of Chittagong and dashed it into the Karnaphuli River Bridge, breaking the bridge in two. The storm destroyed approximately 1 million homes and many boats and small ships in Chittagong harbour, leaving about 10 million people homeless. The storm also struck a hard blow on the Bangladesh military, severely damaging the Bangladesh Navy and Bangladesh Air Force bases there. The storm caused an estimated $ 1.5 billion in damage.

Cyclone Nargis 2008

On May 2, 2008, tropical cyclone Nargis made landfall on Myanmar, formerly known as Burma, and it was the worst natural disaster recorded in the history of the country.

In the early morning of May 2, Cyclone Nargis hit the coast of Myanmar on the Irrawaddy delta at full intensity. Prior to making landfall in Burma (Myanmar), the cyclone intensified to a severe cyclonic storm (equivalent to a category 4 in the Saffir-Simpson scale) with peak winds of 213 km/hr. The storm brought heavy rain, strong winds and a 3.7 m storm surge.

Cyclone Nargis headed up to Yangon, formerly Rangoon, without losing much intensity. Like the Irrawaddy delta, this city is heavy populated. Both of these areas form the majority of the population in Myanmar. The storm weakened as it headed further inland to the Thailand border.

The high winds, rain and the storm surge swept away poorly constructed shacks on the Irrawaddy delta where most of the fertile land is farmed. The storm surge travelled 40 km inland and wiped out villages, killed thousands of people and livestock. With extreme erosion caused by the storm surge, large areas of coastal land were reclaimed by the sea.

The cyclone claimed nearly 140,000 people and another few hundred thousand people went missing. The United Nations estimated that Nargis affected 2.4 million people and rendered thousands families homeless. Nearly 10, 00,000 acres of farmland in Irrawaddy and 3, 00,000 acres in Rangoon division were destroyed. Nargis damaged over 800 000 houses.

HURRICANE

Coringa cyclone, India (1839)

The 1839 Indian cyclone hit Coringa district on November 25, killing 300,000 people and destroying more than 20,000 ships at sea. The 12 m storm surge destroyed the entire city which was then never rebuilt. A cyclone of lesser magnitude had previously hit the same city in 1789 killing 20,000 people. Coringa is now a tiny village of East Godavari district, Andhra Pradesh State in India.

The 1839 Indian cyclone came with extremely powerful winds and torrential rain. The winds produced high waves and damaging storm surge. It caused heavy damage along the coast and significant flooding inland.

Most cyclones develop over the sea and can be noticed weeks before it strikes land. Unfortunately ways of defusing cyclones before they strike land have not been devised. The 1839 Indian cyclone affected such a large area that the population could not be moved away before it struck.

Deadliest hurricanes in history

Cyclone Nargis 2008

On May 2, 2008, tropical cyclone Nargis made landfall on Myanmar, formerly known as Burma, and it was the worst natural disaster recorded in the history of the country.

In the early morning of May 2, Cyclone Nargis hit the coast of Myanmar on the Irrawaddy delta at full intensity. Prior to making landfall in Burma (Myanmar), the cyclone intensified to a severe cyclonic storm (equivalent to a category 4 in the Saffir-Simpson scale) with peak winds of 213 km/hr. The storm brought heavy rain, strong winds and a 3.7 m storm surge.

Cyclone Nargis headed up to Yangon, formerly Rangoon, without losing much intensity. Like the Irrawaddy delta, this city is heavy populated. Both of these areas form the majority of the population in Myanmar. The storm weakened as it headed further inland to the Thailand border.

The high winds, rain and the storm surge swept away poorly constructed shacks on the Irrawaddy delta where most of the fertile land is farmed. The storm surge travelled 40 km inland and wiped out villages, killed thousands of people and livestock. With extreme erosion caused by the storm surge, large areas of coastal land were reclaimed by the sea.

The cyclone claimed nearly 140,000 people and another few hundred thousand people went missing. The United Nations estimated that Nargis affected 2.4 million people and rendered thousands families homeless. Nearly 10, 00,000 acres of farmland in Irrawaddy and 3, 00,000 acres in Rangoon division were destroyed. Nargis damaged over 800 000 houses.

HURRICANE

Coringa cyclone, India (1839)

The 1839 Indian cyclone hit Coringa district on November 25, killing 300,000 people and destroying more than 20,000 ships at sea. The 12 m storm surge destroyed the entire city which was then never rebuilt. A cyclone of lesser magnitude had previously hit the same city in 1789 killing 20,000 people. Coringa is now a tiny village of East Godavari district, Andhra Pradesh State in India.

The 1839 Indian cyclone came with extremely powerful winds and torrential rain. The winds produced high waves and damaging storm surge. It caused heavy damage along the coast and significant flooding inland.

Most cyclones develop over the sea and can be noticed weeks before it strikes land. Unfortunately ways of defusing cyclones before they strike land have not been devised. The 1839 Indian cyclone affected such a large area that the population could not be moved away before it struck.

Test Your MEMORY

1. What is a hurricane?

2. Where did the word hurricane come from?

3. How are hurricanes formed?

4. What is the 'eye' of the hurricane?

5. Write two lines about the eyewall.

6. What are the causes of hurricanes?

7. Write the stages of development of a hurricane.

8. Describe the hurricane categories.

9. Where do hurricanes occur?

10. Who are the hurricane hunters?

11. Write two hurricane safety tips.

12. Name two deadliest hurricanes in history.

Index

B

barometer 10

C

convection cycle 6
coriolis effect 7
counterclockwise 6, 8
cumulonimbus clouds 11

E

El Nino 10
eye 7, 8, 10, 13, 18, 19, 31
eyewall 8, 13, 31

F

flooding 6, 9, 14, 17, 23, 25, 28, 30

H

huracan 5

hurricane hunters 20, 31

I

intensity 13, 14, 19, 20, 29

M

meteorologists 10, 11

N

northern hemisphere 7

R

radiation 6
rip tides 17, 18

S

Saffir-Simpson Hurricane Scale 14
southern hemisphere 7
spiral rainbands 8

spiral storm 3
storms 3, 4, 5, 8, 9, 10, 14, 16, 21, 28
storm surge 12, 14, 15, 17, 26, 28, 29, 30
surface temperature 6

T

tornadoes 4, 17, 18
tropical depression 12
tropical storm 10, 12, 24
tropics 4, 6, 7

W

willy-willies 4